Skinny SIPPER'S

LOW-CALORIE
COCKTAILS

Skinny SIPPER'S

LOW-CALORIE
COCKTAILS

spruce

An Hachette UK Company
www.hachette.co.uk

First published in Great Britain in 2014 by
Spruce, a division of Octopus Publishing Group Ltd
Endeavour House
189 Shaftesbury Avenue
London
WC2H 8JY
www.octopusbooks.co.uk
www.octopusbooksusa.com

Distributed in the US by
Hachette Book Group USA
237 Park Avenue
New York NY 10017 USA

Distributed in Canada by
Canadian Manda Group
664 Annette Street
Toronto, Ontario, Canada M6S 2C8

ISBN 978-1-84601-483-3

A CIP catalogue record for this book is available from the British Library

Printed and bound in China

10 9 8 7 6 5 4 3 2 1

Drinking excessive alcohol can significantly damage your health.
The US Department of Health and Human Sciences recommends
men do not regularly exceed 1–2 drinks a day and women 1 drink.
Never operate a vehicle when you have been drinking alcohol.
Octopus Publishing Group accepts no liability or responsibility for
any consequences resulting from the use of or reliance upon the
information contained herein.

Contents

INTRODUCTION

You've been watching the calories, your weight is perfect, and you feel ready to party. You've never looked or felt better. Then someone tells you how many calories there are in your cocktail…

But how can that be? Cocktails are just liquid! Unfortunately not. Alcohol is fermented sugar, and sugar (as you know) is calories. Add the fruit juices, sugar syrup, cordial, cream, or cola and, before you know it, your Piña Colada is racking up around 280 calories; a Long Island Iced Tea comes in at a shocking 300 or so; and, if a White Russian is your favorite tipple, look away now … up to 375 calories a glass. But don't worry – all is not lost. With a few simple adjustments and some clever substitutions, you can cut the calories without compromising the deliciousness of every sip.

COCKTAIL CALORIES (THE BAD BIT)

In simplest terms, the higher the alcohol content of a liquid, the higher its calorie count, ounce for ounce. As a rule of thumb, spirits that sit around the blow-your-head-off 50 percent alcohol by volume (ABV) mark can contain about 65 calories per shot (a shot is about 1 fl oz or 25 ml), while those at around 40 percent will contain about 55 calories a shot. By way of comparison, a glass of Chardonnay (around 13 percent ABV) contains only about 15 calories per shot (about 140 calories per 5½-fl oz/175 ml glass). This means that inevitably cocktails that use several spirits and super-sweet liqueurs can clock up calories lip-tremblingly quickly.

Sadly, it's not only the alcohol in a cocktail that adds calories. Some cocktails use sugar syrup, which sweetens the bitter taste of spirits, making the drink more delicious, but also more calorific. Standard sugar syrup is a simple dissolution of sugar in water: one teaspoon of sugar contains about 16 calories. Although that seems very little, for every half a shot of sugar syrup you pour into a cocktail, you're also adding about 45 extra calories. Why not try our

PIMM'S CUCUMBER RANGOON P.109

ingenious sugar-syrup alternatives on page 11 instead?

Standard mixers, such as bitter lemon, cola, cordials, and processed fruit juices, all contain high levels of sugar, adding to the overall count. Incidentally, it might surprise you to know that cola contains fewer calories than the same volume of orange juice from concentrate (139 calories as opposed to 158 in a standard can). If you're going to have juice as a mixer, make sure it's freshly squeezed, and that it contains little or no pulp (which adds carbs = sugar = calories).

MAKING IT ALL GOOD

Know your bases. The alcoholic base drink you use in your cocktail will start the ball rolling on how many calories the final drink contains.

True spirits (distilled alcoholic drinks) are kindest on the calories, at least in terms of calories per percentage alcohol. White spirits, such as vodka, white rum, and gin, contain around 55 calories per shot, as does a good-quality 40 percent ABV bourbon, if you prefer your spirits dark. (There will be brand differences, too, so check the labels.) One really happy thought is that dry vermouth contains only around 30 calories per shot – practically a gift from the gods. A couple of those on the rocks will see you in the party mood before you can say "Pass me the canapés."

When choosing your tipple, one thing to think about is that spirits that have been double or triple distilled will have fewer harsh flavors, so there's less need to add calorific liqueurs or mixers to get a delicious result. If you want something unusual, try shochu. This white spirit from Japan looks and tastes like vodka, but can have as few as half the calories — at around 25 calories per shot — depending upon the brand.

If longer sippers are your preference, reach for the fizz. Champagne and prosecco each contain around 130 calories per 5½-fl oz/175-ml standard wine glass. Add a dash of a liqueur (just a dash!), such as Cointreau or crème de cassis, and you could bring this in under 150 calories – just. In general, though, beware liqueurs. Cointreau in fact contains around 85 calories per shot; crème de cassis about 80.

Take the measure of your mixers. All the cocktails in this book that require mixers use the low-cal versions. Sugar-free cola, bitter lemon, and tonic water are the obvious solutions to reducing the calorie intake without compromising on the alcohol. If you need coconut milk (for a Piña Colada, for example), use the reduced-fat kind. Using straight soda water is an absolute must whenever the other flavors will allow. For example, get inventive with your Long Island Iced Tea — try a fruit tea to add a flavor twist and top it with soda water, rather than cola.

Think fresh. Use fresh juices — tomato and carrot juices are your best friends, by the way, at only around 5 to 8 calories per shot. Muddle some fresh berries, rather than using fruit syrup. This will not only give you a natural sugar-boost (it's not calorie-free, but it is lower in calories), it will also boost your antioxidant intake for the day. A low-calorie cocktail with an added health benefit? Have another!

SKINNY EXTRAS

Even if your cocktail is cutting back on the calories, it doesn't have to cut back on the glamor. Some dramatic but low- or no-cal flourishes will make even the skinniest sippers seem utterly decadent. Try adding whole lychees, pomegranate seeds, and olives to the bottom of a martini or short drink; make edible stirrers using celery, carrot, and cucumber sticks for the long drinks that you want to savor.

You can try spicing up the flavor, too — a cinnamon stick (another great stirrer), or some freshly grated nutmeg or muddled ginger will give a spicy kick; a few freshly scraped vanilla seeds will add natural sweetness; spirals of orange, lemon, or lime zest look beautiful and will infuse a citrus zing in your drinks; sprigs of mint and rosemary or even a bay leaf can freshen up that alcohol hit … and all at no extra calories.

PINEAPPLE JULIP P.53

MIXOLOGY MASTERCLASS

Whatever the calorie content of your cocktails, you'll need to know some cocktail basics when it comes to the fine art of mixology.

THE BARTENDER-SPEAK

SHAKE: shaking cocktails means shaking over ice and then straining into a chilled glass. This makes sure the ingredients are properly chilled and combined, and also waters down the hard alcohol hit.

STIR: stirring cocktails gently melds the flavors of the ingredients, usually straight (without ice) or on the rocks (gently stirred through ice).

LAYER: layering involves pouring the ingredients of the cocktail one on top of the other.

MUDDLE: this term refers to grinding or gently squashing fruit or other cocktail ingredients so that they release their flavors into the liquid.

CHURN: this is mixing crushed ice with other cocktail ingredients.

DOUBLE STRAIN: some cocktails need to be strained twice for perfection. The easiest way to do this is by pouring the liquid through the strainer that is attached to your cocktail shaker onto another strainer resting on the glass.

All the cocktails in this book contain 150 calories or fewer and are divided up by drink type – martini, short, long, and shots, poptails, and slushies. Each chapter is subdivided by base spirit, so that you can find something that suits whatever you or your friends fancy. Finally, I know you'll want to know how you can turn the deliciously creamy, but horribly calorific White Russian into something gorgeously silky with fewer than 150 calories. So check out page 91, and enjoy!

WHAT YOU NEED

You don't necessarily need any fancy equipment to make the cocktails in this book, but it's worth knowing which kitchen staples will come in handy when you put on your mixologist's hat. Gather together a fine strainer (such as a sieve or large tea strainer), a paring knife, and a fine grater (such as a microplaner).

Professional cocktail makers will also have a muddler — but you could use a standard pestle — and a long, twisted spoon with a teaspoon measure on one end and a flat top, used to layer drinks. A normal teaspoon will do (you can pour over the back of it to create layers).

We do recommend that you invest in some standard shot measures or a measuring jug, though, as good cocktail-making needs some precision, especially if you're counting the calories.

Of course, having a cocktail shaker

CLICK CLACK SMASH P.98

NOT-SO SUGARY SYRUP

Rather than using a standard sugar syrup, try instead making a syrup using sweetener. Stevia-based powder sweeteners are perfect for this (dissolve 3½ tablespoons of stevia sweetener in 4½ fl oz (125 ml) water and use just as you would for sugar syrup). The calorie results are negligible in your drink. Or you could use agave syrup or nectar. This natural sweetener comes from the sap of the Mexican agave cactus. You can either dilute it 1 part agave syrup to 1 part water and use it exactly as sugar syrup, or don't dilute at all and instead simply half the amount of sugar syrup in each recipe and use undiluted agave instead – either way, using agave you'll halve the calories of normal sugar syrup.

is ideal, but don't go spending a fortune on one. Many cocktails can be made in a pitcher and stirred vigorously. If you do want to shake, try using one of those metal travel coffee mugs (close the top before you shake!), or even a metal vacuum flask, then strain the cocktail through your strainer into a glass. Perfect!

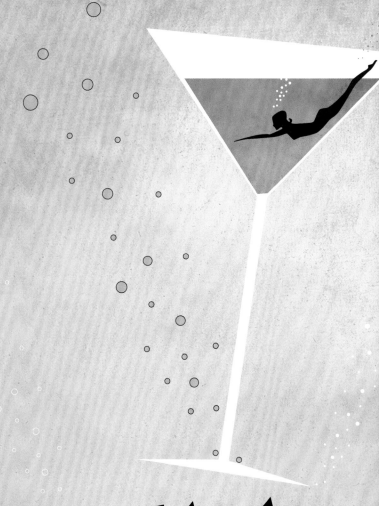

Martinis

145 CALORIES

CLASSIC DRY MARTINI
(PICTURED)

Sometimes called the Naked Martini, this cocktail is far drier than the original Dry Martini.

Makes: 1

½ fl oz (15 ml) dry vermouth

1½ fl oz (35 ml) frozen gin

1 green olive or lemon twist, to decorate

Swirl the vermouth around the inside of a chilled martini glass, then discard the excess. Pour in the frozen gin and add an olive or lemon twist.

145 CALORIES

VESPER

This cocktail, made with a combination of gin and vodka, is prepared by James Bond's method; in other words, it is shaken, not stirred.

Makes: 1

Ice cubes

2 fl oz (50 ml) gin

1 fl oz (25 ml) vodka

½ fl oz (15 ml) Lillet

Lemon twist, to decorate

Put the ice cubes, gin, vodka, and Lillet into a cocktail shaker and shake well. Strain into a chilled martini glass and add a lemon twist.

WHITE LADY
(PICTURED)

Makes: 2

2 fl oz (50 ml) gin

2 fl oz (50 ml) Cointreau

2 fl oz (50 ml) lemon juice

2 lemon twists, to decorate

Pour the gin, Cointreau, and lemon juice into a cocktail shaker. Shake, then strain into two chilled martini glasses, add a twist of lemon to each.

SAPPHIRE MARTINI
(PICTURED PAGE 12)

Makes: 2

8 ice cubes

3 fl oz (75 ml) gin

1 fl oz (25 ml) blue Curaçao

2 red or blue cocktail cherries, to decorate

Put the ice cubes into a cocktail shaker. Pour in the gin and blue Curaçao. Shake well to mix. Strain into two chilled martini glasses, and carefully drop a cherry into each glass.

104 CALORIES

COLLINSON

This recipes uses kirsch, which is an unsweetened clear liqueur distilled from morello cherries and cherry pits.

Makes: 1

3 ice cubes, cracked

1 dash orange bitters

1 fl oz (25 ml) gin

½ fl oz (15 ml) dry vermouth

1½ teaspoons kirsch

Lemon zest

TO DECORATE

½ strawberry

Lemon slice

Put the cracked ice into a mixing glass, then add the bitters, gin, vermouth, and kirsch. Stir well and strain into a chilled martini glass. Squeeze the zest from the lemon rind over the surface of the cocktail, and decorate the rim of the glass with a strawberry half and lemon slice.

145 CALORIES

VODKATINI

Vodka is used instead of gin in this classic recipe. Vodkatinis are usually served very dry.

Makes: 1

1½ teaspoons dry vermouth

2 fl oz (50 ml) frozen vodka

2 green olives or a lemon twist, to decorate

Swirl the vermouth around a chilled martini glass, then pour in the vodka. Finish by adding olives or a lemon rind twist.

149 CALORIES

BELLINITINI

Makes: 1

1½ fl oz (35 ml) vodka

½ fl oz (15 ml) peach schnapps

2 teaspoons peach juice

2 fl oz (50 ml) Champagne, to top up

Peach slice, to decorate

Put the vodka, schnapps, and peach juice into a cocktail shaker and shake well. Pour into a chilled martini glass and top up with Champagne. Decorate with a peach slice.

140
CALORIES

POLISH MARTINI

This is a wonderfully mellow martini made with three different types of Polish vodka with traditional honey and bison grass flavors.

Makes: 2

Ice cubes

2 fl oz (50 ml) Zubrowka vodka

2 fl oz (50 ml) Krupnik vodka

1 fl oz (25 ml) Wyborowa vodka
(standard Polish)

2 fl oz (50 ml) apple juice

Lemon spirals, to decorate

Put the ice cubes into a mixing glass. Pour in the three vodkas and the apple juice, and stir well. Strain into two chilled martini glasses and add a lemon twist.

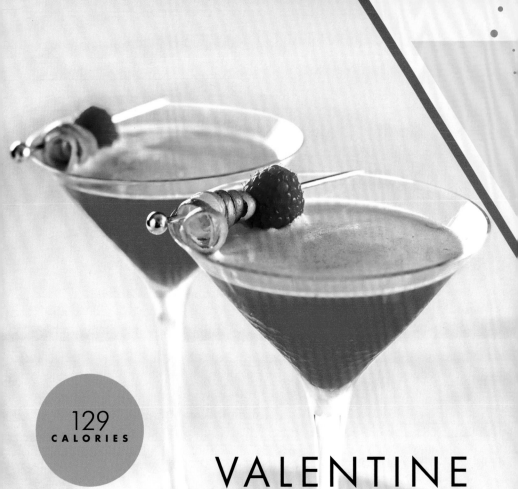

129 CALORIES

VALENTINE MARTINI

Makes: 2

Ice cubes

3½ fl oz (100 ml) raspberry vodka

12 raspberries, plus extra to decorate

1 fl oz (25 ml) lime juice

2 dashes sugar syrup

Lime spirals, to decorate

Half-fill a cocktail shaker with ice cubes. Add all the remaining ingredients and shake until a frost forms on the outside of the shaker. Double-strain into two chilled martini glasses. Decorate with extra raspberries and a lime spiral on toothpicks.

137 CALORIES

STRAWBERRY MARTINI

This cocktail is perfect for early summer drinks in the garden when you can enjoy the wonderful taste of fresh strawberries.

Makes: 1

3 fresh strawberries, hulled, plus ½ strawberry, to decorate

1½ teaspoons sirop de fraises (strawberry syrup)

Ice cubes

2 fl oz (50 ml) vodka

1½ teaspoons dry vermouth

Put the strawberries and sirop de fraises into a mixing glass and muddle together. Transfer to a cocktail shaker, add the ice cubes, vodka, and vermouth and shake well. Strain into a chilled martini glass, decorate with a strawberry half.

140
CALORIES

VANILLA MARTINI

This is a very popular martini, with a soft, mellow flavor from the fresh vanilla.

Makes: 2

2 vanilla pods

3 teaspoons vanilla syrup

4 fl oz (100 ml) vanilla vodka

3 teaspoons dry vermouth

Ice cubes

Put the vanilla pods and vanilla syrup into a mixing glass and muddle together. Add the vanilla vodka, vermouth, and ice cubes and shake well. Strain into two chilled martini glasses.

Short Drinks

GIN TROPICAL

(PICTURED)

There are three different fruit juices to enjoy in this exotic,
low-cal taste of the tropics.

Makes: 1

8 ice cubes

1½ fl oz (40 ml) gin

1 fl oz (25 ml) fresh lemon juice

1 fl oz (25 ml) passion fruit juice

½ fl oz (15 ml) fresh orange juice

Soda water, to top up

Orange spiral, to decorate

Put 4 of the ice cubes into a cocktail shaker, pour in the gin, lemon juice, passion fruit juice, and orange juice and shake well. Put 4 fresh ice cubes into an old-fashioned glass and strain the cocktail over the ice. Top up with soda water and stir gently. Decorate with an orange spiral.

77
CALORIES

BOLERO

Less commonly used than Angostura bitters but a must-have for every
cocktail lover, the ingredients in orange bitters include Seville orange
peel, cardamom, and caraway seeds.

Makes: 1

2 lime wedges

Ice cubes

2 fl oz (50 ml) gin

6 mint leaves

6 drops orange bitters

1 dash sugar syrup

Mint sprig, to decorate

Squeeze the lime wedges into a cocktail shaker. Half-fill the shaker with ice cubes. Add the remaining ingredients and shake until a frost forms on the outside of the shaker. Double-strain into a chilled martini glass, decorate with a mint sprig.

98
CALORIES

129
CALORIES

WATERMELON AND BASIL SMASH

The combination of fragrant basil and sweet, juicy watermelon makes an unusual and refreshing cocktail.

Makes: 1

Ice cubes

2 fl oz (50 ml) gin

3 x ½-inch (1-cm) cubes watermelon

3 basil leaves, plus 1 extra to decorate

2 teaspoons sugar syrup

Add all the ingredients to a cocktail shaker and shake well. Strain into a chilled martini glass, discarding the watermelon chunks and basil leaves. Decorate with a basil leaf floated on the surface of the liquid.

TURF
(PICTURED)

Makes: 2

Crushed ice

2 fl oz (50 ml) gin

2 fl oz (50 ml) dry vermouth

2 teaspoons fresh lemon juice

2 teaspoons Pernod

Lemon slice, to decorate

Put some crushed ice into a cocktail shaker and pour over the gin, vermouth, lemon juice, and Pernod. Shake well, then strain into two glasses containing more ice. Decorate each glass with a lemon slice and straw.

129
CALORIES

BLOSSOM AVENUE

Makes: 1

Crushed ice

1 fl oz (25 ml) Hendrick's gin

2 fl oz (50 ml) rosé wine

2 fl oz (50 ml) apple and rhubarb juice, or cloudy apple juice

1 teaspoon elderflower cordial

Soda water, to top up

TO DECORATE

Kiwi fruit slice

Apple slice

Half-fill a large wine glass with crushed ice, add the gin, wine, apple and rhubarb juice, and elderflower cordial and stir well. Top up with soda water and decorate with a slice of kiwi fruit and a slice of apple.

80
CALORIES

PINK GIN

Angostura bitters, originally intended for medical use, was added to glasses of gin by the British Royal Navy, thus inventing Pink Gin.

Makes: 1

1–4 dashes Angostura bitters
1 fl oz (25 ml) gin
Iced water, to top up

Shake the bitters into a martini glass and swirl around to coat the inside of the glass. Add the gin and top up with iced water to taste, then serve.

78
CALORIES

SALTY DOG

Although traditionally a gin-based cocktail, a Salty Dog can also be made with vodka instead. The rim of the glass can be frosted with salt, like a Margarita, for extra sparkle.

Makes: 1

2–3 ice cubes
Pinch of salt
1 fl oz (25 ml) gin
2–2 ½ fl oz (50–65 ml) fresh grapefruit juice
Orange slice, to decorate

Put the ice cubes into an old-fashioned glass. Put the salt on the ice and add the gin and grapefruit juice. Stir gently and serve, decorated with an orange slice.

CROSSBOW

A skinny winner, this rich-tasting cocktail is a classic combination of chocolate, from chocolate liqueur crème de cacao, and orange-flavored Cointreau.

Makes: 1

4–5 ice cubes

½ fl oz (15 ml) gin

½ fl oz (15 ml) crème de cacao

½ fl oz (15 ml) Cointreau

Drinking chocolate powder, to decorate

Put the ice cubes into a cocktail shaker and add the gin, crème de cacao, and Cointreau. Dampen the rim of a chilled martini glass with a little water, then dip the rim into a saucer of drinking chocolate. Shake the cocktail shaker vigorously, then strain the drink into the glass.

120
CALORIES

115
CALORIES

NEGRONI

An American GI called Negroni stationed in Italy during World War II wanted an extra kick to his Americano cocktail, so the bartender added gin and this cocktail was born.

Makes: 1

Ice cubes

1 fl oz (25 ml) Plymouth gin

1 fl oz (25 ml) Campari

1 fl oz (25 ml) red vermouth

Soda water, to top up (optional)

Orange wedges, to decorate

Put some ice cubes into a mixing glass and fill an old-fashioned glass with ice cubes. Add the gin, Campari, and vermouth to the mixing glass, stir briefly to mix, then strain over the ice in the old-fashioned glass. Top up with soda water, if you like. Decorate with an orange wedges.

147
CALORIES

SLOE GIN SOUR

Makes: 1

Ice cubes

1½ fl oz (35 ml) sloe gin
(damson gin would work just
as well)

¾ fl oz (20 ml) fresh lemon juice

1 egg white

2 teaspoons superfine sugar

Lemon twist, to decorate

Put some ice cubes in a cocktail shaker and add
the gin, lemon juice, egg white, and sugar. Shake
well and strain into a frozen coupette glass, and
top with a lemon twist.

**TIP To freeze your glass, place in the freezer
for about 10–15 minutes.**

132
CALORIES

GINGER SMASH

Makes: 1

1½ fl oz (35 ml) London dry gin

2 teaspoons ginger juice (see
tip on page 80)

¾ fl oz (20 ml) fresh lemon juice

1 teaspoon agave syrup

2 dashes Angostura bitters

Crushed ice

TO DECORATE

Pineapple slice

Orange slice

Pour the gin, ginger and lemon juices, agave
syrup, and bitters into an old-fashioned glass and
muddle. Top up the glass with the crushed ice and
stir well. Decorate with a slice of pineapple and a
slice of orange.

128
CALORIES

HO CHI MINH MARY

Named after Si Racha in Thailand, Srircha chili sauce adds a kick to this twist on the classic Bloody Mary.

Makes: 1

1½ fl oz (35 ml) vodka
3 fl oz (75 ml) watermelon juice
3 fl oz (75 ml) tomato juice
1 teaspoon Srircha chili sauce
1 teaspoon lemon juice
Crushed ice

TO DECORATE
Pineapple slice
Orange slice

Pour the vodka, watermelon, and tomato juices, chili sauce, and lemon juice into an old-fashioned glass and muddle. Top up the glass with crushed ice and stir well. Decorate with a slice of pineapple and a slice of orange.

134
CALORIES

BEETNICK

Agave syrup is one and a half times sweeter than sugar or honey, so you need less of it to sweeten this beautifully hued cocktail.

Makes: 1

1½ fl oz (35 ml) vodka

1 fl oz (25 ml) beetroot juice

1 fl oz (25 ml) orange juice

2 teaspoons lemon juice

1 teaspoon agave syrup

Ice cubes

Orange twist, to decorate

Combine the vodka, beetroot, orange and lemon juices, and agave syrup in a cocktail shaker with some ice cubes. Shake well, until a frost forms on the outside of the shaker, then strain. Pour into a martini glass and decorate with an orange twist.

93
CALORIES

JADE'S JULEP

Naturally high in potassium and low in calories and carbs, coconut water combines with delicate jasmine tea in this fabulous cocktail.

Makes: 1

1 jasmine tea bag
1½ fl oz (35 ml) vodka
Ice cubes
3½ fl oz (100 ml) coconut water
3½ fl oz (100 ml) soda water
1 dash Angostura bitters
Lemon twist, to decorate

Place the tea bag in a wine glass and pour over the vodka. Allow to steep for 2 minutes. Add some ice cubes and the remaining ingredients and stir. Decorate with a lemon twist.

110
CALORIES

ICEBERG

Makes: 1

- 1 sugar cube
- 1 dash Pernod
- 4–6 ice cubes
- 1½ fl oz (40 ml) vodka

Put a sugar cube in an old-fashioned glass, add the Pernod and swirl it around to coat the inside of the glass. Drop in the ice cubes and pour in the vodka. Stir gently to mix.

107
CALORIES

FEDERATION

Makes: 1

- 4–5 ice cubes
- 3 drops orange or Angostura bitters
- 2 fl oz (50 ml) vodka
- 1 fl oz (25 ml) port

Put the ice cubes into a mixing glass. Shake the bitters over the ice. Add the vodka and port. Stir vigorously and strain into a chilled martini glass.

148
CALORIES

HAVEN

Makes: 1

2–3 ice cubes

1 tablespoon grenadine

¾ fl oz (20 ml) Pernod

¾ fl oz (20 ml) vodka

Soda water, to top up

Put the ice cubes into an old-fashioned glass. Dash the grenadine over the ice, then pour in the Pernod and vodka. Top up with soda water and serve with a straw.

142
CALORIES

FRENCH LEAVE

Makes: 1

Ice cubes

1 fl oz (25 ml) orange juice

1 fl oz (25 ml) vodka

1 fl oz (25 ml) Pernod

Put some ice cubes with all the other ingredients into a cocktail shaker and shake well. Strain into a martini glass.

VODKA SAZERAC

Makes: 2

2 sugar cubes
4 drops Angostura bitters
5 drops Pernod
8 ice cubes
3½ fl oz (100 ml) vodka
Diet lemonade, to top up

Put a sugar cube into each old-fashioned glass and shake 2 drops of the bitters over each. Add the Pernod and swirl it around to coat the inside of each glass. Drop 4 ice cubes into each glass and pour in the vodka. Top up with lemonade, stir gently to mix.

134
CALORIES

114
CALORIES

LAILA COCKTAIL

Makes: 1

2 lime wedges

2 strawberries

4 blueberries, plus extra to decorate

1 dash mango puree

1 fl oz (25 ml) raspberry vodka

Ice cubes

Muddle the lime wedges, berries, and mango puree in the bottom of a cocktail shaker. Add the vodka and some ice cubes and shake vigorously. Double-strain into a chilled martini glass and decorate with 3 extra blueberries on a toothpick.

GODMOTHER

(PICTURED PAGE 26)

Makes: 2

8–12 ice cubes, cracked

3 fl oz (75 ml) vodka

1 fl oz (25 ml) Amaretto di Saronno

Put 4–6 cracked ice cubes into each of two old-fashioned glasses. Add the vodka and Amaretto, stir lightly to mix.

VODKA DAIQUIRI

Makes: 1

6 ice cubes, cracked

1 fl oz (25 ml) vodka

1 teaspoon superfine sugar

juice of ½ lime or lemon

Put the cracked ice into a cocktail shaker. Add all the remaining ingredients, shake until a frost forms on the outside of the shaker, and strain into a martini glass.

GINGERSNAP

Makes: 1

4–6 ice cubes

2 fl oz (50 ml) vodka

¾ fl oz (20 ml) ginger wine

Soda water, to top up

Put 4–6 ice cubes into an old-fashioned glass. Pour over the vodka and ginger wine and stir lightly. Top up with soda water.

130 CALORIES

148
CALORIES

SWEET AND CHILI
(PICTURED)

Makes: 2

3 fl oz (75 ml) Scotch whisky

1½ fl oz (35 ml) fresh blood orange juice

1½ fl oz (35 ml) Antica Formula or sweet vermouth

2 teaspoons agave syrup

Ice cubes

1-inch (2.5-cm) red chiles, to decorate

Add the whisky, blood orange juice, Antica Formula or vermouth, and agave syrup to a cocktail shaker with some ice cubes and shake well until a frost forms on the outside of the shaker. Strain into two frozen coupette glasses (see the tip on page 38), decorated with a chile each.

75
CALORIES

NEW YORKER

Makes: 1

2–3 ice cubes, cracked

1 fl oz (25 ml) Scotch whisky

1 teaspoon fresh lime juice

1 teaspoonconfectioners' sugar

½ lemon

Lemon spiral, to decorate

Put the ice cubes into a cocktail shaker and add the whisky, lime juice, and sugar. Shake until a frost forms on the outside of the shaker. Strain into a martini glass, then squeeze the zest from the lemon over the surface and decorate the rim with the spiral.

PINEAPPLE JULEP
(PICTURED)

Taking its name from the French Bourbon dynasty, bourbon is an American whiskey that is a key ingredient in juleps. This spin on the famous Mint Julep (see page 95) adds an Eastern touch with flavors of cardamom and pineapple.

Makes: 1

1½ fl oz (75 ml) bourbon

10 mint leaves

2 teaspoons cardamom syrup [see tip]

2 fl oz (50 ml) pineapple juice

Crushed ice

Pineapple leaves, to decorate

Add the bourbon, mint leaves, cardamom syrup, and pineapple juice to a julep tin or jam jar and churn together. Fill with crushed ice and decorate with a straw and pineapple leaf.

TIP To make the cardamom syrup, steep 20 cardamom pods in 17 fl oz (500 ml) sugar syrup for 48 hours, and strain.

104
CALORIES

CASSIS COCKTAIL

Enjoy berry heaven with a combination of richly sweet and dark blackcurrant liqueur, bourbon, and fresh blueberries.

Makes: 1

4–5 ice cubes

1 fl oz (25 ml) bourbon

½ fl oz (15 ml) dry vermouth

1 teaspoon crème de cassis

2 blueberries, to decorate

Put the ice cubes into a cocktail shaker and pour in the bourbon, vermouth, and crème de cassis. Shake, then strain into a chilled martini glass. Decorate with blueberries on a toothpick.

97
CALORIES

CLUB

Made from the juice of pomegranates and a deep red color, grenadine is a syrup that is an essential ingredient in a range of classic cocktails from Tequila Sunrise to the non-alcoholic Shirley Temple.

Makes: 1

3 ice cubes, cracked

2 dashes Angostura bitters

1 fl oz (25 ml) Scotch whisky

1 dash grenadine

TO DECORATE

Lemon spiral

Cocktail cherry

Put the ice into a mixing glass. Add the bitters, then the whisky and grenadine. Stir well. Strain into a martini glass and decorate with the spiral of lemon and cherry.

90
CALORIES

ROB ROY

Makes: 1

1 ice cube, cracked

1 fl oz (25 ml) Scotch whisky

½ fl oz (15 ml) dry vermouth

1 dash Angostura bitters

Lemon spiral, to decorate

Put the ice cube, whisky, vermouth, and bitters into a mixing glass and stir well. Strain into a martini glass and decorate the rim with the spiral of lemon.

RUSTY NAIL

Makes: 1

Ice cubes

1 fl oz (25 ml) Scotch whisky

1 fl oz (25 ml) Drambuie

Fill an old-fashioned glass with ice cubes. Pour over the whisky and Drambuie and serve.

135 CALORIES

146
CALORIES

HARLEQUIN

Canadian Club Whisky is aged in white oak, giving it a lighter, smoother taste than most Scotches and bourbons. It works particularly well with sweet vermouth in this elegant cocktail.

Makes: 1

5 white grapes, halved

½ fl oz (15 ml) sweet vermouth

6 dashes orange bitters

crushed ice

1½ fl oz (35 ml) Canadian Club Whisky

Put the grapes, vermouth and bitters into an old-fashioned glass. Half-fill the glass with crushed ice, stir well and add the whisky.

87
CALORIES

WHISKY MAC

The full name of this warming cocktail is Whisky Macdonald and it is reputed to have been invented by a Colonel Macdonald serving in India at the time of the British Raj.

Makes: 1

3–4 ice cubes
1 fl oz (25 ml) Scotch whisky
1 fl oz (25 ml) ginger wine

Put the ice cubes into an old-fashioned glass. Pour over the whisky and ginger wine, and stir lightly.

149
CALORIES

OLD- FASHIONED

Short for Old-fashioned Whiskey Cocktail, and with the old-fashioned, or rocks, glass named after it, this is one of those classic cocktails the authentic recipe of which is hotly debated.

Makes: 1

2 fl oz (50 ml) bourbon
Ice cubes
1 teaspoon sugar syrup
4 dashes Angostura bitters
Orange twist, to decorate

Pour the bourbon into an old-fashioned glass and add a few ice cubes. Pour the sugar syrup, then the bitters over the ice. Decorate with an orange twist and serve.

109
CALORIES

RATTLESNAKE

This classic cocktail first appeared in the 1930 edition of the *Savoy Cocktail Book*, the bartending manual of the Savoy Hotel in London.

Makes: 1

4–5 ice cubes, plus extra to serve

1½ fl oz (40 ml) whisky

1 teaspoon fresh lemon juice

1 teaspoon sugar

1 egg white

Few drops Pernod

Put all the ingredients into a cocktail shaker and shake extremely well. Strain into a glass, and add more ice.

119
CALORIES

KICKER

Makes: 1

1 fl oz (25 ml) whisky

1 fl oz (25 ml) Midori

Ice cubes, to serve (optional)

Combine the whisky and Midori in a mixing glass and serve chilled or over the ice cubes.

BOURBON PEACH SMASH

(PICTURED)

Dating back to the late 1800s, the Smash, a classic American cocktail, is enjoying new popularity. This version adds fresh peaches for a sublime taste of summer.

Makes: 2

12 mint leaves

63 peach slices

6 lemon slices, plus extra to decorate

3 teaspoons superfine sugar

3½ fl oz (100 ml) bourbon

Ice cubes

TO DECORATE

2 mint sprigs

2 lemon slices

Muddle the mint leaves, peach and lemon slices, and sugar in a cocktail shaker. Add the bourbon and some ice cubes and shake well. Pour over fresh ice into two old-fashioned glasses. Decorate with a mint sprig and a lemon slice.

65
CALORIES

ASTRONAUT

Makes: 1

8–10 ice cubes

½ fl oz (15 ml) white rum

½ fl oz (15 ml) vodka

½ fl oz (15 ml) fresh lemon juice

1 dash passion fruit juice

Lemon wedge, to decorate

Put 4–5 ice cubes into a cocktail shaker and add the rum, vodka, lemon, and passion fruit juices. Fill an old-fashioned glass with 4–5 fresh ice cubes. Shake the drink, then strain it into the glass. Decorate with the lemon wedge.

149
CALORIES

CUBA LIBRE

Legend has it that this famous cocktail was invented in Cuba in the 1800s as a way for soldiers to get away with drinking alcohol – the cola and lime apparently disguised the rum.

Makes: 1

Ice cubes

2 fl oz (50 ml) golden rum, such as Havana Club 3-year-old

Freshly squeezed juice of ½ lime

Diet cola, to top up

Lime wedges, to decorate

Fill an old-fashioned or highball glass with ice cubes. Pour over the rum and lime juice and stir. Top up with diet cola, and decorate with lime wedges and straws.

116
CALORIES

84 CALORIES

MELON DAIQUIRI

Makes: 1

2 fl oz (50 ml) white rum
1 fl oz (25 ml) fresh lime juice
2 dashes Midori
2 scoops crushed ice

Put the white rum, lime juice, and Midori in a blender with the crushed ice and blend until smooth. Pour into a chilled goblet and decorate with straws.

125 CALORIES

STRAWBERRY DAIQUIRI

Makes: 1

1 fl oz (25 ml) white rum
½ fl oz (15 ml) crème de fraises
½ fl oz (15 ml) fresh lemon juice
4 fresh strawberries, hulled
Crushed ice

TO DECORATE
Strawberry slice
Mint sprig

Put the rum, crème de fraises, lemon juice, strawberries, and ice in a food processor or blender and process at a slow speed for 5 seconds, then at high speed for about 20 seconds. Pour into a chilled glass and decorate with a strawberry slice and a mint sprig.

HOPPER'S FIX
(PICTURED)

127 CALORIES

Makes: 1

1½ fl oz (35 ml) dark rum

1 fl oz (25 ml) espresso (cooled to room temperature or chilled)

½ teaspoon chocolate hazelnut spread

Ice cubes

3 coffee beans, to decorate

Put the rum, espresso, and chocolate hazelnut spread in a cocktail shaker. Muddle the ingredients well in order to dissolve the chocolate hazelnut chocolate spread. Add several ice cubes and shake well until a frost forms on the outside of the shaker. Strain, then pour into a martini glass. Decorate with the coffee beans floated in a cluster on the surface.

BACARDI COCKTAIL

144 CALORIES

In 1936, a New York State Supreme Court ruled it illegal to make this cocktail without using Bacardi rum.

Makes: 1

Ice cubes

2 fl oz (50 ml) Bacardi white rum

¾ fl oz (20 ml) fresh lime juice

½ fl oz (15 ml) grenadine

Lime spiral, to decorate

Half-fill a cocktail shaker with ice cubes. Add all the remaining ingredients and shake until a frost forms on the outside of the shaker. Strain into a chilled martini glass and decorate with a lime spiral.

RUM OLD-FASHIONED

(PICTURED)

Makes: 1

3 ice cubes

1 dash Angostura bitters

1 dash lime bitters

½ teaspoon superfine sugar

½ fl oz (15 ml) water

2 fl oz (50 ml) white rum

½ fl oz (15 ml) dark rum

Lime wedge, to decorate

Stir 1 ice cube with the bitters, sugar and water in a heavy-based old-fashioned glass until the sugar has dissolved. Add the white rum, stir, and add the remaining ice cubes. Add the dark rum and stir once again. Decorate with a lime wedge.

149
CALORIES

ASTRAL WEEK

Makes: 1

1½ fl oz (35 ml) white rum

½ lime, cut into small wedges

5 x 1-inch (2.5-cm) cubes watermelon

1 teaspoon agave syrup

6 mint leaves

Crushed ice

Kiwi fruit slice, to decorate

Add the rum, lime, watermelon, agave syrup and mint leaves to an old-fashioned glass and muddle. Top up the glass with crushed ice and stir. Top with a kiwi fruit slice.

149
CALORIES

ST CLEMENTS COLLINS

Makes: 1

1 citrus tea bag
1½ fl oz (35 ml) white rum
Ice cubes
2 teaspoons lemon juice
1 teaspoon superfine sugar
Soda water, to top up
Lemon or orange twist, to decorate

Place the tea bag into a wine glass and steep in the rum for 2 minutes. Discard the tea bag and add some ice cubes to the glass. Add the remaining ingredients, stir, and decorate with a twist of orange or lemon.

103 CALORIES

PINK TREASURE

119 CALORIES

Makes: 1

2 ice cubes, cracked

1 fl oz (25 ml) white rum

1 fl oz (25 ml) cherry brandy

Diet bitter lemon or soda water, to taste (optional)

Lemon spiral, to decorate

Put the cracked ice, rum, and cherry brandy into a glass. Add a splash of bitter lemon or soda water, if using. Decorate with a lemon spiral.

FLORIDA SKIES

59 CALORIES

Historically known, among other names, as kill-devil, Barbados water, and Nelson's blood, rum – particularly white or light rum – is a key ingredient for every mixologist.

Makes: 1

3 ice cubes, cracked

1 fl oz (25 ml) white rum

1½ teaspoons lime juice

½ fl oz (15 ml) pineapple juice

Soda water, to top up

Lime or cucumber slice, to decorate

Put the cracked ice cubes in a Collins glass. Pour the rum, lime juice, and pineapple juice into a cocktail shaker. Shake lightly. Strain into the glass and top up with soda water. Decorate with the slice of lime or cucumber.

126
CALORIES

COCONUT AND LIME MARGARITA

Made from the blue agave plant, tequila is distilled in the area surrounding the town of Tequila in the Mexican state of Jalisco. The very best to be had is 100 percent agave tequila.

Makes: 2

Ice cubes

3 fl oz (75 ml) 100 percent agave tequila

4 teaspoons lime cordial

4 teaspoons coconut syrup

3 fl oz (75 ml) pineapple juice

1 fl oz (25 ml) lime juice

2 lime wheels, to decorate

Combine the ingredients in a cocktail shaker and shake well until a frost forms on the outside of the shaker. Strain and pour into two martini glasses, and decorate with a lime wheel.

CAIPIRINHA

This is a variation of a cocktail from Brazil, made from cachaça – a blend of rum and sugar cane.

Makes: 1

6 lime wedges

2 teaspoons brown sugar

2 fl oz (50 ml) cachaça

4–5 ice cubes, crushed

Place 3 of the lime wedges in a large tumbler or old-fashioned glass and add the brown sugar and cachaça. Mix well, mashing the limes slightly to make a little juice. Top up with the crushed ice cubes, and decorate with the remaining lime wedges.

145 CALORIES

BITTER SPRING

131
CALORIES

Makes: 1

Ice cubes

2 fl oz (50 ml) Aperol

2 fl oz (50 ml) fresh orange juice

2 fl oz (50 ml) pink grapefruit juice

2 fl oz (50 ml) soda water

Grapefruit wedge, to decorate

Half-fill an old-fashioned glass with ice cubes, pour over the remaining ingredients, and stir. Serve decorated with a grapefruit wedge.

SPANISH COBBLER

114
CALORIES

Makes: 1

1 teaspoon superfine sugar

2 fl oz (50 ml) dry sherry

2 pineapple wedges

2 orange wedges

2 mandarin wedges

2 lemon wedges

Crushed ice

TO DECORATE

Pineapple or orange slice

Combine the sugar and sherry in a mixing glass and stir until the sugar is dissolved. Add the fruit wedges and muddle. Finally, top with crushed ice and stir. Pour into an old-fashioned glass and decorate with a pineapple or orange slice.

Long
Drinks

TANQSTREAM

Makes: 2

Cracked ice cubes

3½ fl oz (100 ml) Tanqueray gin

¾ fl oz (20 ml) lime juice

5 fl oz (150 ml) soda water or diet tonic water

¾ fl oz (20 ml) crème de cassis

TO DECORATE

Lime slices

Mixed berries

Put some cracked ice with the gin and lime juice into a cocktail shaker and shake to mix. Strain into two highball glasses, each half-filled with cracked ice. For a dry Tanqstream, add soda water; for a less dry drink, add tonic water. Stir in the crème de cassis, and decorate with the lime slices and mixed berries.

132 CALORIES

DELFT DONKEY

109
CALORIES

Makes: 1

3–4 ice cubes, cracked
2 fl oz (50 ml) gin
Juice of 1 lemon
Diet ginger beer, to top up
Lemon slice, to decorate

Put the cracked ice into a cocktail shaker and pour over the gin and lemon juice. Shake until a frost forms on the outside of the shaker. Pour into a hurricane or other large glass. Top up with ginger beer. Decorate with a lemon slice and serve with a straw.

GIN FLORADORA

120
CALORIES

The Floradora takes its name from a musical comedy that was one of the first successful Broadway musicals of the 20th century, and famous for its chorus line of "Floradora Girls".

Makes: 1

4–5 ice cubes
½ teaspoon sugar syrup
Juice of ½ lime
½ teaspoon grenadine
2 fl oz (50 ml) gin
Diet dry ginger ale, to top up
Lime twist, to decorate

Put the ice cubes into a cocktail shaker. Pour the sugar syrup, lime juice, grenadine, and gin over the ice and shake until a frost forms on the outside of the shaker. Pour without straining into a hurricane glass. Top up with dry ginger ale, and decorate with a lime twist.

117
CALORIES

CHAMOMILE GARDEN

Makes: 1

1½ fl oz (35 ml) London dry gin

2 dashes peach bitters

2 fl oz (50 ml) apple juice

2 fl oz (50 ml) chamomile tea, chilled

Juice of ½ lime

10 mint leaves

Crushed ice

Soda water, to top up

TO DECORATE

Peach slice

Mint sprigs

Add the gin, bitters, apple juice, tea, lime juice, and mint leaves to a sling glass. Stir and then fill the glass with crushed ice, churn, and top up with the soda water. Decorate the glass with a peach slice and some mint sprigs.

VIBE ALIVE
(PICTURED)

Makes: 1

2 grapefruit wedges

2 lime wedges

1 teaspoon Orgeat syrup

1½ fl oz (35 ml) gin

Ice cubes

Sugar-free energy drink, to top up

Combine the grapefruit, lime wedges, and the syrup in a highball glass and muddle together. Add the gin and stir well. Add several ice cubes, top up with the energy drink, decorate with a straw, and stir well.

132
CALORIES

GINGER RICKY

Makes: 1

4 x 1-inch (2.5 cm) cubes
pineapple

1½ fl oz (35 ml) London dry gin

½ fl oz (15 ml) ginger juice
(see tip)

1 teaspoon lime juice

Ice cubes

3½ fl oz (100 ml) diet dry
ginger ale

Pineapple leaf, to decorate

Muddle the pineapple in a cocktail shaker, then add the gin and ginger and lime juices. Shake well, strain, and pour into a Collins glass filled with ice cubes. Top up with the ginger ale and decorate with a pineapple leaf.

TIP To make ginger juice, peel a large piece of fresh ginger and blitz in a blender or food processor. Strain the juice before use.

129
CALORIES

SWEET SIXTEEN

146
CALORIES

Makes: 1

6–8 ice cubes

2 fl oz (50 ml) gin

Juice of ½ lime

2 dashes grenadine

1 teaspoon sugar syrup

Diet bitter lemon, to top up

Lemon rind strip, to decorate

Put half the ice cubes into a cocktail shaker and pour over the gin, lime juice, grenadine, and sugar syrup. Shake until a frost forms. Put the remaining ice cubes into a highball glass, strain the cocktail over the ice, and top up with bitter lemon. Decorate with a lemon rind strip.

ALBEMARLE FIZZ

109
CALORIES

Tanqueray gin was originally distilled in 1830 by Charles Tanqueray in London. It is renowned for its distinctively smooth, lingering taste.

Makes: 1

4–6 ice cubes

1 fl oz (25 ml) Tanqueray gin

Juice of ½ lime

2 dashes raspberry syrup

½ teaspoon sugar syrup

Soda water, to top up

2 cocktail cherries, to decorate

Put half the ice cubes into a mixing glass and add the gin, lemon juice, and raspberry and sugar syrups. Stir to mix, then strain into a highball glass. Add the remaining ice cubes and top up with soda water. Decorate with the cherries impaled on a toothpick and straws.

BERRY COLLINS

(PICTURED)

Makes: 1

4 raspberries, plus extra to decorate

4 blueberries

1 dash strawberry syrup

Crushed ice

2 fl oz (50 ml) gin

2 teaspoons fresh lemon juice

1 teaspoon sugar syrup

Soda water, to top up

Put the berries and strawberry syrup into a highball glass and muddle together. Fill the glass with crushed ice. Pour over the gin, lemon juice, and sugar syrup, stir well and top up with soda water. Decorate with the extra raspberries.

99
CALORIES

EARL'S TONIC

Earl Grey tea, made with the oil of the fragrant bergamot orange fruit, gives this zesty cocktail a distinctive and unforgettable flavor.

Makes: 1

1 Earl Grey tea bag

1½ fl oz (35 ml) London dry gin

3½ fl oz (100 ml) diet tonic water

2 fl oz (50 ml) pink grapefruit juice

Ice cubes

Pink grapefruit slice, to decorate

Place the tea bag in a Collins glass and pour over the gin. Allow to steep for 2 minutes, then discard the tea bag. Add the other ingredients and stir well to combine. Decorate with a slice of pink grapefruit.

143
CALORIES

PIMM'S COCKTAIL

First produced in London in 1823 by James Pimms, gin-based, herb-infused Pimm's No. 1 Cup captures the essence of English summer.

Makes: 2

Ice cubes

2 fl oz (50 ml) Pimm's No. 1 Cup

2 fl oz (50 ml) gin

3½ fl oz (100 ml) diet lemonade

3½ fl oz (100 ml) diet ginger ale

TO DECORATE

Cucumber strips

Blueberries

Orange slices

Fill two highball glasses with ice cubes. Add the remaining ingredients, one by one in order, over the ice. Decorate with cucumber strips, blueberries, and orange slices, and serve.

TOM COLLINS

Makes: 2

3½ fl oz (100 ml) gin

½ fl oz (15 ml) lemon juice

2 teaspoons sugar syrup

Ice cubes

Soda water, to top up

Lemon slices, to decorate

Divide the gin, lemon juice, and sugar syrup between two highball glasses. Stir well and fill the glasses with ice cubes. Top up with soda water, add a lemon slice to each glass.

121
CALORIES

131
CALORIES

WHITE CUCUMBER FIZZ

Makes: 1

4–6 ice cubes

2 fl oz (50 ml) white wine

1 fl oz (25 ml) citrus vodka

2 fl oz (50 ml) cucumber juice (see tip)

2 teaspoons elderflower cordial

2 fl oz (50 ml) soda water

Lemon wedge or cucumber slice, to decorate

Place all the ingredients in a cocktail shaker. Shake well until a frost forms on the outside of the shaker. Pour into a Collins glass and decorate with a lemon wedge or cucumber slice.

TIP To make cucumber juice, peel a medium cucumber and then process it in a blender or juicer. Strain the juice before use.

POM COLLINS

Half-fill a highball glass with ice cubes, add all the other ingredients and stir. Decorate with a lime wedge.

Makes: 1

Ice cubes

1 fl oz (25 ml) vodka

2 fl oz (50 ml) pomegranate juice

2 fl oz (50 ml) fresh apple juice

2 teaspoons elderflower cordial

Lime wedge, to decorate

VODKA, LIME AND SODA

Makes: 1

Ice cubes

1 fl oz (25 ml) vodka

2 fl oz (50 ml) lime cordial or lime juice

Soda water, to top up

Lime slice, to decorate

Half-fill a Collins glass with ice cubes. Pour in the vodka and lime cordial or lime juice, top up with soda water, and stir. Decorate with a lime slice.

HAIR RAISER

Makes: 2

6–8 ice cubes, cracked

2 fl oz (50 ml) vodka

2 fl oz (50 ml) sweet vermouth

2 fl oz (50 ml) diet tonic water

Lemon and lime spirals, to decorate

Put 3–4 cracked ice cubes into 2 highball glasses and pour over the vodka, vermouth, and tonic water. Stir lightly, decorate with the lemon and lime spirals, and with straws.

90
CALORIES

147
CALORIES

PASSIONATA

(PICTURED)

Adding the pulp and seeds of passion fruit gives a luscious tart, yet sweet, note to this very grown-up cocktail.

Makes: 1

1½ fl oz (35 ml) vodka

2 fl oz (50 ml) cranberry juice

1 passion fruit, halved

Ice cubes

Sugar-free energy drink, to top up

Combine the vodka and cranberry juice in a highball glass. Scoop out the flesh from one half of the passion fruit and add this to the glass. Add several ice cubes to the glass and stir until well combined. Top up with the energy drink, and decorate with the other half of the passion fruit.

140
CALORIES

SKINNY RUSSIAN

Makes: 1

Ice cubes

1 fl oz (25 ml) coffee liqueur, such as Tia Maria

1 fl oz (25 ml) vodka

2½ fl oz (65 ml) unsweetened almond milk

Fill a tumbler with some ice cubes, then pour in the coffee liqueur and vodka. Give it a stir. Keep stirring slowly as you pour in the almond milk to combine completely.

LE MANS
(PICTURED)

Makes: 1

2–3 ice ice cubes, cracked

1 fl oz (25 ml) Cointreau

½ fl oz (15 ml) vodka

Soda water, to top up

Lemon slice, to decorate

Put the ice into a Collins glass. Add the Cointreau and vodka, stir, then top up with soda water. Float the lemon slice on top.

86
CALORIES

RICKEY

Makes: 1

4–5 ice cubes

1½ fl oz (40 ml) whisky

1½ fl oz (40 ml) fresh lime juice

Soda water, to top up

Lime twist, to decorate

Put the ice cubes into a highball glass. Pour over the whisky and lime juice. Top up with soda water and stir. Decorate with a lime twist.

105
CALORIES

135
CALORIES

J W APPLE COOLER

Makes: 1

Ice cubes

1½ fl oz (35 ml) Johnnie Walker
Gold Label Reserve

3½ fl oz (100 ml) pressed apple
juice

2 teaspoons fresh lemon juice

4 dashes lemon bitters

Mint sprig, to decorate

Fill a Collins glass with ice cubes, add all the
other ingredients, and stir well to combine.
Decorate with a mint sprig.

TIP If you find the cocktail too sour, add up
to a teaspoon of sugar syrup, but remember
that this will add approximately 15 calories.

MINT JULEP

This is the ultimate cocktail of America's Deep South. The earliest written reference dates this aperitif back to 1803.

Makes: 1

10 mint leaves, plus an extra sprig to decorate

1 teaspoon sugar syrup

4 drops Angostura bitters

Crushed ice

2 fl oz (50 ml) bourbon

Put the mint leaves, sugar syrup, and bitters into a highball glass and muddle together. Fill the glass with crushed ice. Pour over the bourbon and stir well. Decorate with a mint sprig and serve.

MOROCCAN JULEP

Makes: 1

1 peppermint tea bag

1 green tea bag

1½ fl oz (35 ml) white rum

6 mint leaves

1 teaspoon agave syrup

Ice cubes

3½ fl oz (100 ml) soda water

Cucumber slice or lemon slice, to decorate

Place the peppermint and green tea bags in a Collins glass and pour over the white rum. Allow to steep for 3 minutes, then discard the tea bags. Add the steeped rum, mint leaves, and agave syrup to a cocktail shaker. Shake and strain over ice cubes into a Collins glass, then top up with soda water. Stir well and decorate with a cucumber or lemon slice.

149
CALORIES

APPLE-SOAKED MOJITO

Mint and apple are a match made in heaven in this fresh take on the enduring summery classic that is the Mojito.

Makes: 1

1½ fl oz (35 ml) white rum

10 mint leaves

¾ fl oz (20 ml) fresh lime juice

2 teaspoons superfine sugar

1½ fl oz (35 ml) pressed apple juice

Crushed ice

Apple fan or apple slice, to decorate

Combine the rum, mint leaves, lime juice, sugar, and apple juice in a sling glass and muddle until well combined. Fill the glass with crushed ice and churn. Decorate with an apple fan or apple slice.

TIP Squeeze lemon juice over the apple slice to stop it turning brown.

MOJITO

Makes: 2

16 mint leaves, plus sprigs to decorate

1 lime, cut into wedges

4 teaspoons granulated sugar

Crushed ice

4 fl oz (100 ml) white rum

Soda water, to top up

Muddle the mint leaves, lime, and sugar in the bottom of two highball glasses and fill with crushed ice. Add the rum, stir, and top up with soda water. Decorate with mint sprigs and serve.

145 CALORIES

121
CALORIES

CLICK CLACK SMASH

Spicy fresh ginger and cardamom are mixed with fresh pineapple and warming rum in this icy winner cocktail.

Makes: 1

1½ fl oz (35 ml) white rum

2 green cardamom pods

¼ lime, cut into wedges

2 thumbnail-size pieces of fresh ginger, peeled

5 pineapple wedges

1 teaspoon agave syrup

Crushed ice

Add the rum, cardamom pods, lime, ginger, 4 of the pineapple wedges, and agave syrup to a Collins glass and muddle. Fill with crushed ice and churn, then crown with more crushed ice. Decorate with the remaining pineapple wedge.

PINK RUM

(PICTURED)

Makes: 1

3 drops Angostura bitters

3–4 ice cubes

2 fl oz (50 ml) white rum

2 fl oz (50 ml) cranberry juice

1 fl oz (25 ml) soda water

Lime slice, to decorate

Shake the bitters into a highball glass and swirl it around. Add the ice cubes, then pour in the rum, cranberry juice, and soda water. Decorate with a lime slice.

149
CALORIES

ST JAMES

Makes: 1

3–4 ice cubes

Juice of ½ lime or lemon

Juice of 1 orange

3 drops Angostura bitters

2 fl oz (50 ml) white or golden rum

2 fl oz (50 ml) diet tonic water

Lime or lemon slice, to decorate

Put the ice cubes into a highball glass and pour in the lime or lemon juice and the orange juice. Shake the bitters on the ice, add the rum and tonic water, stir gently, and decorate with a lime or lemon slice.

138
CALORIES

121
CALORIES

JALISCO
(PICTURED)

Makes: 1

Crushed ice

1½ fl oz (35 ml) tequila

4 inch (10 cm) slice cucumber

1 cilantro (coriander) sprig

2 teaspoons lime juice

4 pineapple wedges

1 teaspoon agave syrup

Icecubes

TO DECORATE

Twist of black pepper

Cucumber slice

Add all ingredients to a blender or food processor with some ice cubes and blend until well combined. Pour into a Collins glass and top with black pepper and a cucumber slice.

86
CALORIES

FLORECIENTE

Makes: 1

1 orange slice

Fine sea salt

Crushed ice

1 fl oz (25 ml) tequila gold

¾ fl oz (20 ml) Cointreau

¾ fl oz (20 ml) fresh lemon juice

¾ fl oz (20 ml) fresh blood orange juice

Blood orange wedge, to decorate

Frost the rim of a large old-fashioned glass by moistening with the orange slice, then pressing the glass into a saucer of salt. Fill the glass with crushed ice. Pour the tequila, Cointreau, lemon juice, and blood orange juice into a cocktail shaker, shake vigorously for 10 seconds, then strain into the prepared glass. Decorate with a blood orange wedge.

PALOMA

Spanish for "dove," this Mexican cocktail rivals the popularity of its more famous sister, the Margarita, in its country of origin.

Makes: 1

2 teaspoons fresh lime juice

1 teaspoon salt

1½ fl oz (35 ml) 100 percent agave tequila

3½ fl oz (100 ml) fresh pink grapefruit juice

1 fl oz (25 ml) soda water

Ice cubes

Wet the rim of a highball glass with a little of the lime juice, spread the salt out in a saucer, and dip the moistened rim of the glass into it to create a salt crust around the rim. Add the remaining ingredients and some ice cubes to the glass, and stir well.

HORSE'S NECK

(PICTURED)

Makes: 1

3 ice cubes, cracked

1½ fl oz (40 ml) brandy

Diet ginger ale, to top up

Lemon spiral, to decorate

Put the ice into a Collins glass and pour over the brandy. Top up with ginger ale. Decorate with the lemon spiral.

89 CALORIES

TIDAL WAVE

(PICTURED PAGE 74)

Makes: 1

6 ice cubes

1 fl oz (25 ml) Mandarine Napoléon

3½ fl oz (100 ml) diet bitter lemon

1 dash fresh lemon juice

Lemon slice, to decorate

Put the ice cubes into a highball glass. Add the Mandarine Napoléon, bitter lemon, and lemon juice and stir well. Decorate with a lemon slice.

84
CALORIES

PIMM'S CUCUMBER RANGOON

(PICTURED)

For hot and hazy days, this sweet sipper blends long-lived classic Pimm's No. 1 Cup with cooling cucumber juice and tangy ginger ale.

Makes: 1

2 fl oz (50 ml) Pimm's No. 1 Cup

2 fl oz (50 ml) cucumber juice (see tip on page 87)

3½ fl oz (100 ml) diet dry ginger ale

Ice cubes

TO DECORATE

Cucumber strips

Blueberries

Orange slices

Pour all the ingredients into a Collins glass filled with ice cubes. Stir well and decorate with cucumber strips twisted around the edge of the glass, orange slices, mint sprigs, blueberries and a straw.

85
CALORIES

BRANDY CUBAN

Makes: 1

2–3 ice cubes

1½ fl oz (40 ml) brandy

Juice of ½ lime

Diet cola, to top up

Lime slice, to decorate

Place the ice cubes in a tumbler and pour over the brandy and lime juice. Stir vigorously to mix. Top up with cola and decorate with a slice of lime and a straw.

Shots, Poptails, & Slushies

POPPY

Makes: 2

Ice cubes

1½ fl oz (40 ml) vodka

2 dashes Chambord

2 teaspoons pineapple puree

Put some ice cubes into a cocktail shaker, add the vodka, Chambord, and pineapple puree and shake briefly. Strain into two shot glasses.

60 CALORIES

43
CALORIES

BASIL VICE

Makes: 1

2 basil leaves
Crushed ice
½ fl oz (15 ml) vodka
1 dash raspberry syrup

Roll the basil leaves up tightly, cut into thin strips, and chop very finely. Place them in the bottom of a shot glass, then almost fill the glass with crushed ice. Pour on the vodka. Stir and add a dash of raspberry syrup.

85
CALORIES

DANGEROUS DETOX

Makes: 1

½ fl oz (15 ml) peach schnapps
½ fl oz (15 ml) cranberry juice
½ fl oz (15 ml) vodka
1 dash absinthe

Carefully pour the ingredients into a shot glass in order of density, as listed in the ingredients, so that you have three equal layers and a thin green line of absinthe at the top.

65
CALORIES

ROCK CHICK

Schnapps is a clear liquor distilled from fermented fruit. The five types of fruit used to make schnapps are apples, pears, cherries, apricots, and peaches.

Makes: 1

Ice cubes

1 fl oz (25 ml) Absolut Kurant Vodka

1 dash peach schnapps

1 dash fresh lime juice

Half-fill a cocktail shaker with ice cubes. Add all the remaining ingredients and shake briefly to mix, then strain into a shot glass.

71
CALORIES

KAMIKAZE

Developed in the 19th century and originally called Curaçao triple sec, triple sec is a colorless, orange-flavored variety of Curaçao.

Makes: 1

6 ice cubes, cracked

½ fl oz (15 ml) vodka

½ fl oz (15 ml) triple sec

½ fl oz (15 ml) fresh lime juice

Put the cracked ice into a cocktail shaker. Add all the remaining ingredients and shake until a frost forms on the outside of the shaker, then strain into a shot glass.

RUDE JUDE

78
CALORIES

Makes: 1

Ice cubes

1 fl oz (25 ml) white rum

1 dash strawberry puree

1 dash strawberry syrup

1 dash fresh lime juice

Put some ice cubes into a cocktail shaker and pour over the rum, strawberry puree and syrup, and lime juice. Shake well and strain into a shot glass.

SPICED BERRY

78
CALORIES

Morgan Spiced Rum has a mellow, spicy flavor and is named after 17th-century Welshman, Sir Henry Morgan, a Caribbean pirate.

Makes: 1

Ice cubes

1 fl oz (25 ml) Morgan Spiced Rum

1 dash fresh lime juice

1 dash raspberry puree

1 dash sugar syrup

Put some ice cubes into a cocktail shaker and pour over the rum, lime juice, raspberry puree, and sugar syrup. Shake briefly and strain into a chilled shot glass.

78
CALORIES

TEQUILA SLAMMER

Makes: 2

2 fl oz (50 ml) tequila gold

2 fl oz (50 ml) chilled Champagne

Pour the tequila into two shot glasses. Slowly top up with the Champagne. Cover the top of the glass with the palm of your hand to seal the contents inside and grip it with your fingers. Briskly pick up the glass and slam it down on a surface to make the drink fizz. Quickly gulp it down in one, while it's still fizzing.

122
CALORIES

PAPA G

Makes: 2

Ice cubes

2 fl oz (50 ml) Amaretto di Saronno

2 dashes lemon juice

2 dashes sugar syrup

2 drops Angostura bitters

Put some ice cubes in a cocktail shaker, add the other ingredients and shake briefly. Strain into two shot glasses.

PASSION SPAWN

(PICTURED PAGE 110)

86
CALORIES

Makes: 2

Ice cubes

2 fl oz (50 ml) silver tequila

2 dashes triple sec

2 dashes lime juice

2 passion fruit

Put some ice cubes in a cocktail shaker, add the tequila, triple sec, and lime juice and shake well. Strain into two chilled shot glasses. Cut the passion fruit in half and squeeze the pulp over the shots to decorate.

DASH LOVE

Makes: 2

¾ fl oz (20 ml) light crème de cacao

1¼ fl oz (30 ml) chilled tequila

4–6 drops raspberry puree

Pour the crème de cacao into 2 shot glasses. Using the back of a bar spoon, slowly float the chilled tequila over the crème de cacao. Carefully add the raspberry puree to the surface of the liquid — it should sink and then float midway.

149 CALORIES

BLOODY SIMPLE

55 CALORIES

Pepper or chili vodka and Tabasco sauce give this shot a fiery aftertaste, and a peppery tomato wedge adds fuel to the fire.

Makes: 1

1 fl oz (25 ml) chilled pepper or chili vodka

2–3 drops Tabasco sauce

Pepper

Celery salt

Tomato wedge

Pour the vodka into a shot glass, then add the Tabasco sauce. Mix some pepper and celery salt together on a small saucer. Dip the tomato wedge into the pepper and salt mixture to lightly coat, then eat after drinking the shot.

69 CALORIES

RED VELVET

If you can't find any fresh plums, this would work nicely with peaches or nectarines, too.

Makes: 8

¼ cup (50 g) superfine sugar

2 plums, quartered and pits removed

1 fl oz (25 ml) gin

1 fl oz (25 ml) Grand Marnier

9 fl oz (250 ml) diet ginger ale

Place the sugar, plums, and 4 fl oz (120 ml) water in a saucepan. Bring slowly to a boil and allow to bubble for 5–10 minutes until the plums are completely soft. Let cool completely. Place the cooled plums and syrup in a blender or food processor and blitz until smooth. Pass through a fine strainer and stir in the rest of the ingredients. Pour into eight icepop molds. Place the molds in the freezer. Let set for 2 hours, insert the icepop sticks, and freeze until solid (about 4 more hours).

119
CALORIES

POMEGRANATE, VANILLA, AND VODKA

This is best made with a vanilla pod as you get flecks of seeds through the poptail, but if you can't get your hands on any, replace with 1 teaspoon vanilla extract (no need to allow it to infuse).

Makes: 4

½ vanilla pod

¼ cup (50 g) superfine sugar

12 fl oz (350 ml) pomegranate juice

2 fl oz (65 ml) vodka

Scrape the seeds from the vanilla bean and place both pod and seeds in a saucepan with the sugar and 5 fl oz (125 ml) water. Slowly bring to a boil, allowing the sugar to dissolve. Let simmer gently for 5 minutes, then remove from the heat. Allow to infuse for 30 minutes. Remove the vanilla pod from the syrup and mix in the pomegranate juice and vodka. Pour into ice-cube trays and place in the freezer. Let set for 2 hours or until slightly set before serving.

113
CALORIES

PASSION FRUIT MARGARITA

When removing the seeds from the passion fruit, be sure not to lose any of the delicious juice.

Makes: 6

½ cup (125 g) superfine sugar

Grated zest of 1 lime

½ cup (125 ml) passion fruit pulp (about 6 passion fruit)

3 fl oz (75 ml) lime juice

1 fl oz (25 ml) tequila

½ fl oz (15 ml) Cointreau

Place the sugar and lime zest in a small saucepan with 250 ml (9 fl oz) water. Slowly bring to a boil, allowing the sugar to dissolve. Let bubble 5 minutes, then remove from the heat. Stir in the remaining ingredients and pour into 6 icepop molds. Place the molds in the freezer. After 3 hours give each one a gentle stir to distribute the passion fruit seeds and insert the icepop sticks. Return to the freezer for an additional 3 hours, until frozen solid.

102
CALORIES

STRAWBERRY COSMOPOLITAN

The strawberries are crushed rather than blended, which gives this slushie a very satisfying texture that is just delicious.

Makes: 4

¼ cup (50 g) superfine sugar

1 cup (200 g) hulled and quartered strawberries

1 fl oz (25 ml) vodka

1 fl oz (25 ml) Cointreau

4½ fl oz (125 ml) soda water

Place the sugar and 4½ fl oz (125 ml) water in a small saucepan. Let the sugar dissolve over low heat, then bring it to a boil. Remove from the heat. Add the strawberries to the pan. Squash the strawberries into the syrup using the back of a fork or a pestle, but allowing some texture to remain. Pour in the remaining ingredients and pour the whole mixture into an ice-cube tray. Freeze for 2 hours or until almost solid, the blend briefly to make a slush.

ACKNOWLEDGMENTS

PICTURE CREDITS

Alamy M. Brauner/Bon Appetit 107. Octopus Publishing Group Jonathan Kennedy 4, 6, 8, 9, 11, 30, 33, 41, 50, 53, 65, 68, 71, 79, 80, 90, 98, 102, 105, 108; Lis Parsons 121, 122, 125; Neil Mersh 101; Stephen Conroy 12, 15, 17, 19, 21, 22, 25, 26, 37, 45, 47, 49, 55, 57, 61, 62, 67, 72, 76, 83, 85, 86, 89, 93, 97, 110, 112, 118; William Reavell 29, 35, 74.

Publisher Sarah Ford
Additional Recipes and Styling Allan Gage and Felix von Nida
Nutritionist Angela Dowden
Editor Pauline Bache
Designer Eoghan O'Brien and Geoff Fennell
Picture Library Manager Jennifer Veall
Production Controller Sarah Connelly